A Letter to My Future Stepson

A Letter to My Future Stepson

Getting Started Investing

Joe M. Thomason

© 2017 Joe M. Thomason
All rights reserved.

ISBN: 1979557608
ISBN-13: 9781979557603

CONTENTS

Introduction · vii

Chapter 1 The Letter · 1

Chapter 2 Definitions · 13

Chapter 3 Questions · 20

Chapter 4 Conclusion · 26

INTRODUCTION

Recently, my fiancée's son told her that he wanted to start thinking about stock market investing, and he wanted to pick my brain on the topic. I've gotten to know him a bit over the last couple of years, and he's a terrific young man in his early twenties, serving our great country in the US Air Force. I was delighted that he'd be interested in considering my advice, especially since it's a subject I'm greatly interested in. I got to thinking about all there is to know about the stock market and the vast amount of information and variety of opinions out there on the topic. Geez, where to start? I decided I'd just write him a letter providing a brief summary or outline of the investing concepts I consider to be the most important. If he wanted to keep things pretty simple, this letter could possibly be all he needed to know. If he decided to get a bit more advanced, it would provide a good starting point with recommended reading and other resources for expanding his knowledge.

I started dabbling in investing when I was around his age, but I really had no idea what I was doing. I had heard that it was wise to invest in quality mutual funds and hope for steady long-term gains. That sounded like a boring get-rich-slow method, and since I was young and thought I knew it all, I wanted to get rich quick. When I was starting out, I would just hear about how a company might be doing something good or new or exciting and just jumped in and bought some shares of it. I sometimes did OK, but I usually lost money. In some cases, I lost a lot of money, or at least what seemed like a lot to me at the time.

I realized the hard way that companies I thought of as being successful didn't necessarily possess the traits likely to make their stock shares increase in price. I also learned that the condition of the general market is a huge—maybe the biggest—factor in how well a stock performs. You can buy shares in a profitable, growing, and groundbreaking company, but if the general market is going down, there is a good possibility that company will go down with it. I should also mention that the condition of a company's sector (e.g., Microsoft = technology, Chevron = energy, etc.) is also a big factor in how a stock's price moves, and sometimes a sector will move differently than the general market. Many of the poor investment decisions of my younger years were made when I didn't have much money to lose, and I should have been concentrating on paying off debts or building an emergency fund. To quote one my favorite get-out-of-debt gurus Dave Ramsay, "Sometimes we have to pay some stupid tax."

Luckily, we have the opportunity to learn from our mistakes and improve. Every time I've made mistakes investing in the stock market, I've done some contemplating, reading, and studying, and I learned something. I later learned to abandon knee-jerk stock buys and embrace a more diversified, long-term buy-and-hold approach, which turned out to be much wiser and more effective. Later still, I learned to implement some of the concepts of trend following to sidestep market downturns and improve gains, and I've been pretty pleased with this approach. Even better than learning from our mistakes is learning from someone else's mistakes. Maybe this booklet, combined with some of the other books and resources I've recommended, can serve that purpose.

You might ask yourself, "Who is this guy and why should I care about his investing advice to his future stepson?" If you're looking for advice from someone who works at a fancy Wall Street firm and makes huge commissions pushing his firm's products, I'm not your guy. If you'd like to hear from an average working guy who's made a lot of mistakes, learned a lot from trial and error, studied lots of advice from various experts, and is finally making some progress in beefing up funds for his retirement, then you might want to give this quick read some consideration. I was pretty proud of how the letter to my future stepson turned out and felt it did a good job of cutting through much of the confusion and mysticism of the stock market and simplifying it a bit. I decided to turn my letter into a short book and put it out there in hopes that it would be helpful to others as well. I hope you find it helpful and enjoyable.

CHAPTER 1
THE LETTER

Your mom told me you were thinking about getting started in investing and didn't know where to start. Here are some pointers I've picked up over the years through lots and lots of reading and trial and error. I'm now forty-one years old and just starting to feel like I'm becoming a pretty good investor. Maybe I can save you from some of the many mistakes I've made.

Strongly Recommended Prerequisites for Getting Started
I strongly recommend having paid off all your debts other than your house. I also strongly recommend an emergency fund of six months' living expenses, separate from your investment account. If you're anxious to get started learning and practicing investing with a small portion of your budget, maybe there's a bit of flexibility if you feel really strongly about job stability. If your disposable income is $1,000 a month (or $100, $500, etc.), maybe half could go toward your investment account and half could go to accelerating debt payoff or building up your emergency fund. That's just an idea; it's really best to have your debts paid off and a complete six-month emergency fund first as described in Dave Ramsay's book *Total Money Makeover*.

Important Pitfall to Avoid
You need to know this from the beginning. It took me many mistakes to figure this out, and I would be way ahead now if I had known this when

I started. Absolutely avoid acting on impulse and buying stocks based on "tips" from friends, coworkers, news articles, and so forth. Instead, feel free to observe, learn, and think about "what if" you had bought this stock with imaginary money. Wait until after you fully understand the investment strategy described in step 3B (discussed below), and then you can consider a tip something to do some further research on but not act on immediately.

Getting Started

Step 1: Start an investment savings plan

Go ahead and thoroughly review your budget and decide how much you can put into an investment account each month or per paycheck or every other paycheck, whatever works best for your budget situation. It's important to stick to this amount once you've gotten started; the emergency fund helps keep you from needing to use your investment money on unexpected house, car, or other problems. Those things will happen often. They're not that bad if you're prepared.

Step 2: Open and set up a trading account

This is similar to a regular bank account, but you can use it to buy, hold, and sell securities, such as stocks, mutual funds, ETFs, bonds, etc.

Let's take a quick pause to go over some definitions you might not know.

Mutual fund: a fund or grouping of many stocks (hopefully good stocks) that helps you diversify and spread out your risk. In mutual funds, an active manager tries to pick top stocks and create a good return.

Pros and cons of mutual funds
Pros: many funds reduce risk and produce a nice, steady return (maybe an average of 12–16 percent over a ten-year period for the good ones).

A LETTER TO MY FUTURE STEPSON

Cons: The often-high fees (a few percentage points) can cut into that nice, steady return. Many managers don't pick that well and fail to beat the general market. For example, the S&P 500 is a stock market index that measures the US stock market and is frequently mentioned on the financial news. Over the last five years, the S&P 500 averaged 14.38 percent; some mutual funds beat that, some funds didn't, and many funds didn't after management fees.

There are thousands of mutual funds to choose from, and picking one can be a challenge. A good way to start is to use the research tools on your trading account platform (Schwab or the website of the company that you set up an account with). Morningstar.com has good information, and there's also some good stuff on Yahoo Financial.

ETF (exchange-traded fund): I prefer these. Similar to mutual funds but not actively managed, their fees are far lower (often less than 1 percent), and they trade easily like a stock. They still represent many stocks but can be focused into certain sectors. These are often called index funds. For example, there are many ETFs that represent the S&P 500. The most well known is the Spyder 500, commonly referred to by its ticker symbol, SPY, and regularly mentioned in the financial news. If you had invested in SPY over the last five years, the return would have been very close to the 14.38 percent I mentioned earlier. There are several that represent the Dow Jones, the NASDAQ, and the Russell 2000 indexes.

There are also many ETFs that represent various types of bonds; small, medium, and large companies; dividend-paying stocks; specific sectors, such as construction, energy, health care, and technology; international, small countries, big countries, specific countries—there are tons. You can research them the same way you do mutual funds on your brokerage account website, on Morningstar.com, in financial articles, et cetera. If the number of choices seems daunting, I recommend concentrating on funds or ETFs from Schwab, Vanguard, or Fidelity. They have low fees and a great reputation for client-first mentality. You might find hidden gems at other fund families as well.

Where to set up your account
I recommend Charles Schwab. They have a reputation for putting the client first and lots of resources to help you. You can look up a wealth of information on their website. You gain access to far more information after you set up your account and log in, including many how-to articles and webinars. There are also very friendly advisors you can call if you need to ask a question.

I've also heard good things about Vanguard and Fidelity; you might also consider looking into TD Ameritrade, Scottrade, E*TRADE, T. Rowe Price, or others. I use OptionsXpress. It is a division of Charles Schwab that allows options trading. I believe some of the regular Charles Schwab accounts now allow this, too. I experimented with options trading some when I was younger and lost a lot of money. I realized the hard way that options are extremely volatile and risky. I don't recommend them, especially if you're not single and have others depending on you.

There are several types of accounts from which to choose. I'd recommend a Roth IRA, a regular IRA, and a regular trading account. The first two have tax advantages, but there is a penalty for making withdrawals before age fifty-nine. There are also some accounts designed to give tax breaks on college funds for any future college students you might have. I'm not sure how those work; you could ask a CPA if you're interested. You might just want to pick one type of account to start out with and add more as your budget, investing experience, and tax situation evolve.

Step 3: Investment strategies

A: Long-term buy-and-hold strategy
It's a lot like it sounds. You contribute money to your investment brokerage account, buy quality diversified mutual funds and/or ETFs, and shoot for steady long-term gains.

A LETTER TO MY FUTURE STEPSON

Pros: Dave Ramsay recommends this strategy. It's best for most people, best to start with, and what most people use in their company 401(k)s and pensions.

Cons: It requires patience and persistence. (Most investing strategies do.)

There are many different theories on the best way to do it. (This is a con of almost all investment strategies.)

The major weakness with this strategy is that you are subjected to market downturns, including severe downturns like the ones in 2001–2003 and in 2007–2009, in which the market went down as much as 50 percent.

Traditionally, the stock market has recovered from these downturns stronger than ever, but it's very scary when it's happening. This chart helps put it in perspective.

Chart 1—SPY, the ETF that follows the S&P 500

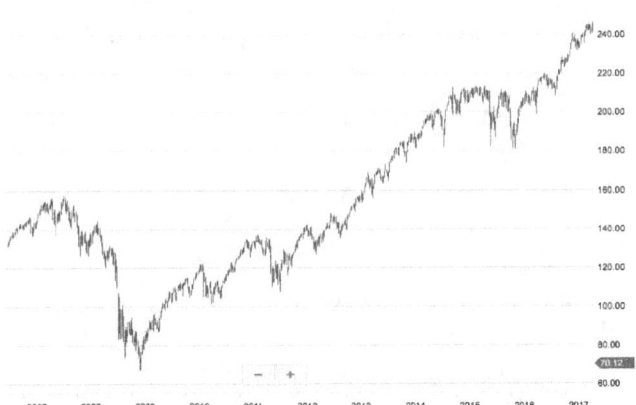

What if you had bought $500 worth of mutual funds and/or ETFs that tend to follow the S&P 500 toward the end of 2007? A year later, it would have been worth around $200–250, and you'd likely have been worried sick throughout 2008. You wouldn't have fully regained your loss until 2013.

5

However, buy-and-hold gurus will tell you that if you had faith in the market recovering and kept buying a consistent amount every month or so on the way down, you would have taken advantage of the concept of dollar-cost averaging (being able to buy more and more shares as the market falls, which will be much more valuable when the market comes back up). If you had done this throughout 2008 and 2009, today you'd be sitting pretty with some nice average overall gains in your account.

I used to use this method, and I usually think it's not a bad idea for most people, but a fear nags at me in the back of my mind. What if the next major downturn doesn't recover? What if it shoots down like in 2001–2003 and 2007–2009 and just stays down? Many say this isn't possible, but it's happened in other countries with increasing levels of socialism and government has taken over. Our economy in the United States has traditionally been very strong and able to recover from downturns because of limited government, reasonably low taxes, a strong currency, a reasonably free market, and a pro-capitalist mentality. What if that's not always the case? Or if that sounds too crazy, what if the recovery is so slow that I need to retire or have a family disaster that requires money during that downturn? It might not happen that way, but that's why I later studied up on the methods we'll be talking about in step 3B. Before I get to that, here is a sample portfolio of ETFs you might use in a long-term buy-and-hold strategy.

US growth stocks: VTI Vanguard Total Stock Market (Usually hot companies like Apple, Google, Netflix, Amazon, etc.)	20 percent
US stocks—growth and income: SCHD Schwab Dividend Equity (Usually older, larger, steadier companies like Johnson & Johnson and Wal-Mart)	20 percent
US stocks—international: VT Vanguard International (Hot international companies like Alibaba, the Chinese Amazon)	20 percent

Real estate investment trusts: VNQ Vanguard REIT (Companies that invest in real estate and convey most of their profits as dividends)	20 percent
Bond market (or cash): BND Vanguard Total Bond Market (Loans and bonds, such as US treasury bonds. Small and steady returns—maybe 1–4 percent—possibly not as safe as they once were)	20 percent

If a major downturn happened, and you had faith it would eventually recover, you might use some of that bond money (hopefully small but steady returns) or cash and buy more in the other categories at discount prices.

Recommended Reading
Total Money Makeover, by Dave Ramsey, is simple but good.

MONEY: Master the Game, by Tony Robbins, contains a wealth of information. It's a huge book, but you can scan through or skip much of it, such as the sections on annuities. The author also repeats himself at times.

There is another point of interest in the buy-and-hold strategy you want to consider, and that is the magic of compounded interest. Over long periods of time, maybe fifteen- to twenty-year periods, the stock market has averaged about 8 percent on the S&P 500 index and 11 percent on the NASDAQ index. Let's say your balanced portfolio averages 10 percent. (Some years you may make 20 percent, and some years may be at –5 percent, but you average out to 10 percent over a long period.)

Let's say you start to dabble in investing at age twenty-five, but maybe you get greedy, make a few mistakes, and drain your account for some unexpected life disasters. Maybe it takes a while to get debts paid off or emergency fund built up, and you don't really get started until you're thirty. (This will also make for simpler math.) Let's say you decide you'd like to fully or partially retire at age sixty, giving you thirty years of investing.

Here are some possible scenarios:

Example 1

> Age 30–60
> $500 per month into investing account
> 10 percent average return
> Value of account at age 60: $1,130,244
> Withdraw 5 percent per year: $56,512
> (Financial advisors recommend that you not withdraw more than 5 percent per year to make your funds last.)

This might not be too bad if all your debts are paid off, but remember, inflation will have driven prices of everything up, and you might have big vacations you want to take or grandkids to spoil, and so forth.

What if you upped your monthly input?

Example 2

> Age 30–60
> $1,000 per month into investing account
> 10 percent average return
> Value of account at age 60: $2,260,488
> Withdraw 5 percent per year: $113,024

Not bad.

What if you are on a tighter budget and you can only afford $250 a month?

Example 3

> Age 30–60
> $250 per month into investing account
> 10 percent average return
> Value of account at age 60: $565,122
> Withdraw 5 percent per year: $28,258

This could possibly be a good supplement if you had other income from another source such as a pension but I wouldn't want to try to live off that.

What if we can only do $250 a month, but we delay our retirement to age sixty-five and contribute five more years?

Example 4

> Age 30–65
> $250 per month into investing account
> 10 percent average return
> Value of account at age 65: $949,160
> Withdraw 5 percent per year: $47, 458

The extra five years of contributions makes a big improvement.

What if we use the same scenario, but we get pretty good at investing and are able to average 14 percent gains?

Example 5

> Age 30–65
> $250 per month into investing account
> 14 percent average return
> Value of account at age 65: $2,775,738
> Withdraw 5 percent per year: $138,787

I'd call that pretty good!

As you can see, any increases to the monthly investment amount, the number of years investing, or the average return percentage can amount to a significant increase in the amount you end up with. If you were able to maximize all three areas you could make yourself, your family, and your favorite charities really darn prosperous. That's why it's called the *magic* of compound interest.

B: Trend-following strategy

What exactly is trend following? In a nutshell, imagine a roller coaster: hop on when it's headed up, and hop off when it's headed down.

Pros: It provides the ability to sidestep downturns, especially major downturns, and to increase returns, maybe from 8–12 percent to 15–25 percent or more.

Cons: There's a lot to learn. This strategy requires regular monitoring, oftentimes daily. You're likely to make some mistakes while learning. You must sometimes incur some small losses to avoid big losses, and you sometimes have to jump into and out of the market.

The market gives lots of fake-outs. It looks like it's changing directions—going down only to immediately turn back up or vice versa. I'm getting older and can't afford to lose much anymore, so I decided to learn this strategy because the two pros for me far outweigh all the cons. It is also possible (and recommended) to implement a hybrid strategy, in which you use a diversified buy-and-hold-type portfolio like the example shown previously and monitor the market direction. Hop out when it's going down; hop back in when it's going up.

Here is an example of how you might do that with an ETF:

Chart 2—SPY: early August 2016 to early August 2017

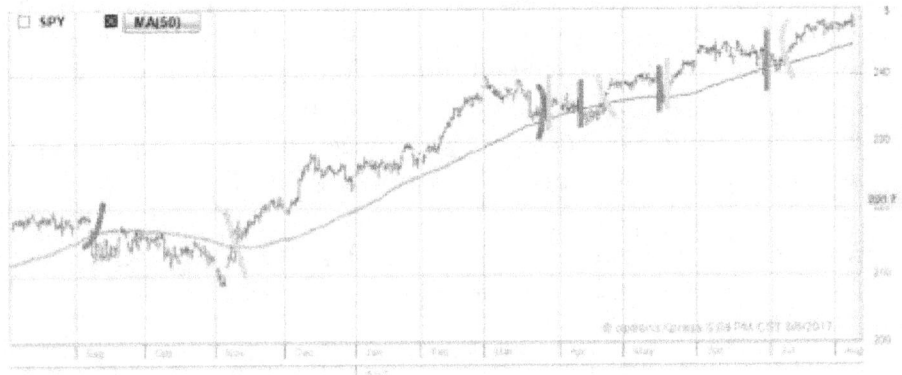

Chart 3—SPY: early August 2016 to early August 2017

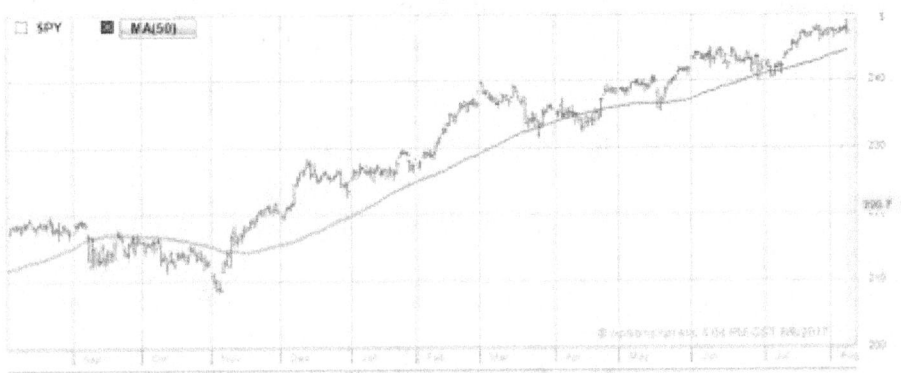

Chart 2 is a one-year chart of SPY (S&P 500 ETF). It covers from early August 2016 to early August 2017. The darker marked-in lines show when to get out; the lighter marked-in lines show when to get back in. How did I know? When the stock dips below its fifty-day moving average, I get out. When the stock price crosses back above its fifty-day moving average, I get back in.

The fifty-day moving average (represented here by the left to right, upward trending line) is the average of the closing stock price on each of the previous fifty days. It shows the general direction the stock is heading by evening out the normal daily fluctuations, helping you put things in perspective. It is also common to hear about five-, ten-, fifteen-, twenty-, thirty-, one-hundred-fifty-, and two-hundred-day moving averages, all doing the same thing to a lesser or greater degree.

You'll notice there are occasions when I get out and then get right back in; I call those market fake-outs.

Chart 3 is the same chart without the lines, just so you can see it more clearly.

You might think, "Why bother?" Remember the *big* downturn in chart 1? Imagine the peace of mind of sidestepping that and not losing money while that is happening.

Like I said, for me the pros outweigh the cons.

You can do this with ETFs as shown above or with top-rated growing stocks that are set to go up in price in an up-trending market. The best way to learn how to do this is to read *How to Make Money in Stocks* by William O'Neil. It's a big book but goes fast because it's so interesting and full of illustrations. Keep your Internet search engine nearby to explain difficult words or concepts. After you've got that read and studied a bit, subscribe to *Investor's Business Daily* (IBD), the ultimate trend-following stock investor's resource, at Investors.com. There are also lots of helpful learning tools and information on there.

Additional recommended reading includes *Secrets for Profiting in Bull and Bear Markets*, by Stan Weinstein, and *How I Made $2,000,000 in the Stock Market*, by Nicholas Darvas. There is also a great blog called wishingwealthblog.org.

May the force be with you!

CHAPTER 2
DEFINITIONS

Since this letter was intended for someone with minimal investing experience, I'll include some additional definitions and investing concepts.

Bid/ask price: You'll notice these two prices displayed when you enter an order to buy or sell a stock. At any given time while the market is openly trading, the bid price is roughly what you can sell the stock for, and the ask price is roughly what you can buy the stock for. Keep in mind that, from the time you enter the trade order into the computer to the time the trade is executed, the price can vary a bit.

Bond: A debt investment in which an investor loans money to an entity, which borrows the funds for a defined period of time at a variable or fixed rate. Corporations, municipalities, the US federal government, and foreign governments issue bonds to raise money. You can also find mutual funds and ETFs that track certain types of bonds or combinations of different types of bonds.

For further information on how bonds work, check out some interesting free lessons on the educational website Khanacademy.com.

Bull market/bear market: A bull market is when the general market is rising and stock prices, on average, are going up. A bear market is just the opposite. You can identify a bull market on the stock chart of a major market index such as the S&P 500 when the two-hundred-day moving average is moving in a slightly upward direction, and the fifty-day moving average is above the two-hundred-day moving average, also moving in a slightly upward direction. A bear market is just the opposite. If the stock or index price moves below the fifty-day moving average, and the fifty-day moving average begins to move downward toward the two-hundred-day moving average, you could say the market is under pressure. This could mean the bull market is transforming into a bear market, or it could just be a temporary slowdown (or pullback).

Day order versus good-until-canceled order: A day order is only effective the day you place the order or the following day if you place the order in the evening after trading hours. If your order is not filled that day, it is automatically canceled. A good-until-canceled order stays in effect until either it is filled or you cancel it. I normally use a day order to buy a stock and a good-until-canceled order for a stop-loss sell order.

Dividends: When companies are profitable, they might choose to use their profits for growth, expansion, hiring, et cetera, or they might choose to pay out a portion of those profits to their shareholders in the form of a dividend. Oftentimes, a company that pays a dividend is a larger, more established, and steadier type of company. For example, Wal-Mart (WMT) is currently (2017) paying a dividend of $0.51 per share per quarter or $2.04 per year.

Dividend yield: A dividend expressed as a percentage return rate. Dividend yield is calculated by dividing the annual dividend by the stock price. For example, Wal-Mart (WMT) has a current dividend of $2.04 per year and a current stock price of $79 per share. The dividend yield is 2.58 percent (2.04/79 = 2.58 percent).

Dividend dates: When investing in a stock that pays dividends, some dates you want to consider are the announce date, the ex-dividend date, and the payment date. The announce date is the date on which the board of directors announces there will be a dividend. The ex-dividend date, sometimes called the ex-date, is important because you must have owned the stock prior to this date to receive dividends. Payment date is of course when the dividends are paid; they are usually credited to your trading account.

Dow Jones: The Dow Jones Industrial Average, commonly referred to as the Dow, is a popular index used to gauge how the stock market is doing. It uses only thirty stocks to monitor the market, but these are very large and well-known companies. Large, reliable, and well-known companies like these are commonly known as blue-chip companies. These are companies that are traded on the New York Stock Exchange. If you like the idea of investing in this type of company, you could invest in an ETF that reflects the Dow, such as SPDR Dow Jones (DIA).

Earnings per share (EPS): This is very much like it sounds: earnings (or profits) divided by the number of shares a company has outstanding. Companies report their earnings every quarter. An investor looking to make money in growth stocks will want to find companies that are growing their earnings from year to year and quarter to quarter and are expected to continue doing so.

ETFs: Exchange-traded funds. Similar to mutual funds in that they represent a group of stocks but not actively managed, their fees are usually far less (often less than 1 percent) than a mutual fund, and they trade easily like a stock. ETF's often reflect certain sectors or a certain index. These are often called index funds. A discussion of these is found in the letter under "getting started."

Exchange-traded products (ETPs): An ETP would be a broader category than an ETF. A common type of ETP is an ETF, but not all of these products are funds that represent a group of stocks or bonds. Sometimes they represent a commodity, such as crude oil; a currency; or a precious metal, such as gold.

Fundamental analysis: A method of security valuation that examines a company's financial and operational information, including sales, earnings, growth, growth potential, assets, debts, management, products, and competition.

Leveraged ETFs: These are ETFs that are designed to move at a certain multiple, usually two or three times, of a certain index. For example, the Proshares Ultra QQQ (QLD) is considered a double-leveraged ETF and designed to move twice as much as the Powershares NASDAQ (QQQ). The Proshares Ultrapro QQQ (TQQQ) is considered a triple-leveraged ETF and therefore designed to move three times as much as QQQ. These are very volatile and risky and should only be used with extreme caution.

Market capitalization: Market capitalization (or market cap) refers to the market value of all the company's shares. A company with a market cap of more than $10 billion is typically referred to as large cap, $300 million to $2 billion would be small cap, and mid cap would fall right in the middle. Large-cap companies are typically steady, reliable, proven performers. Small-cap companies have room to grow and are likely looking to do so. Some achieve this, and some fail. Mid cap is the middle of both worlds. Many ETFs and mutual funds will concentrate on tracking either large-, mid-, or small-cap companies.

Market order versus limit order: A market order directs your broker to buy or sell a stock or other security at the best price currently available. A market order is unrestricted, so if the market for a stock is changing rapidly, you could end up with a different price than you expected. This could be for better or worse. A limit order specifies a price you will not go over if buying or under if selling. This can protect you from an unexpected price deviation but can also limit your ability to quickly unload or pick up a security. I picture it like an auction environment, where several people are shouting out what they're willing to take or give for an item; however, in this case, much of the process is handled electronically.

Mutual fund: a fund or grouping of many stocks that helps you diversify and spread out your risk. In mutual funds, an active manager tries to pick top stocks and create a good return. The best mutual fund managers are able to pick the best stocks and beat the returns of the general market. It has been estimated that only about the top 5 percent of mutual funds are able to consistently beat the market. Mutual funds have been criticized in recent years for charging management fees that are too high.

NASDAQ: When someone mentions the NASDAQ, he or she might be referring to the all-electronic US stock exchange where more than a billion shares a day are traded. He or she might also be referring to the NASDAQ Composite, which is an index that tracks the stocks traded on—you guessed it—the NASDAQ. NASDAQ stocks are more likely to be technology or Internet stocks but not necessarily. A popular ETF that tracks many of the top stocks on the NASDAQ is the Powershares QQQ (QQQ). The NASDAQ index will typically outperform the Dow and S&P over longer periods of time, but it moves up and down more rapidly.

Options: A stock option is the right to buy or sell a stock at a certain price. A call option is the right to buy a stock at a certain price, and a put option is the right to sell a stock at a certain price. A trader looking to gain from an upward movement in a stock's price would buy call options, and a trader looking to gain from a stock's downward movement in price would use put options. A small movement in a stock's price can equate to a much larger price movement in an option to buy that stock. While the possibility of magnified gains can be very enticing, the possible losses are also magnified. Options also expire and become worthless after a certain amount of time. The magnified volatility coupled with the impending expiration date makes options trading a very risky and advanced strategy.

Price per earnings or P/E ratio: This gives investors an idea of value by taking a company's price and dividing it by the EPS. A value investor might look for bargains by comparing a company's P/E ratio with those of similar stocks.

Russell 2000: You don't hear about this index nearly as much, but sometimes you might. This index tracks some of the smallest companies traded on the exchanges. There are several ETFs that track the Russell 2000. One of the more common ones is BlackRock iShares (IWM).

Selling short: This is a technique used by traders looking to profit from a security they believe is going to go down in price. You effectively sell shares of a stock you don't have by borrowing them. Then, after the shares drop in price, you buy them back (called buy to cover), keeping the diffcrence. Of course, that's what you hope will happen. The stocks can also go up in price, and you'd have to come up with more money to buy them back. This is a very risky and advanced strategy. Stocks and the market in general can show many signs of moving into a downturn only to quickly reverse back up.

S&P 500: The Standard and Poor's 500 also tracks the stock market, but it is generally considered more all encompassing than the Dow since it tracks five hundred leading companies instead of thirty. A popular ETF that tracks this index is the SPDR S&P 500 (SPY).

Stock: A share of ownership in a company held by an individual or group. Corporations raise capital by issuing stocks that entitle shareholders to partial ownership of the company. The most typical form is common stock; common stock includes voting rights, which allow shareholders to vote on major issues being decided by the corporation at the annual shareholders meeting. Common stock also entitles shareholders to dividends, if there are any, and is usually easy to transfer or sell. There is also preferred stock, which functions more like a bond. Preferred stock ranks above common stock in the event of a corporate bankruptcy or liquidation but does not include voting rights. When you hear about someone buying or selling a stock, it is usually common stock. Stocks are also sometimes called equities.

Stop order: Also called a stop, a stop-loss, or a stop-on quote, this is a stock order that triggers the sale (or purchase) of a stock when it reaches a certain price. If you bought a stock at one hundred dollars per share but want to be sure to cut your losses and get out if it drops below ninety dollars per share, you could set a stop-loss order to trigger the sale if your stock drops below the ninety-dollar mark. This order will trigger automatically if you are away from your computer and unable to keep a constant eye on your stock. This is a very useful and important tool that I strongly recommend using.

Technical analysis: A method of evaluating stocks and other securities by studying patterns on charts that indicate price trends and volume data. An example of this method would be the trend-following example I shared in chart 2 in the original letter. Trend following is a type of technical analysis.

Note: One of the main reasons I like and recommend *Investor's Business Daily* is that it does a very effective job of reporting information on stocks, mutual funds, ETFs, and general market conditions using a combination of fundamental and technical analysis.

Value Investing: This is an investing style that uses fundamental analysis to find stocks with impressive or at least potentially impressive fundamentals that are selling for a bargain price. A value investor might review profits, assets, and other factors related to a certain stock and decide the stock should be worth one hundred dollars per share. If it currently is selling on the market for fifty dollars per share, it is a potential bargain. This style of investing is often associated with Warren Buffett. *The Intelligent Investor* by Benjamin Graham is considered one of the best books on this topic.

CHAPTER 3
QUESTIONS

A few questions occurred to me after I wrote the letter, and I thought it might be helpful to include them here.

I heard from friends that the company they work for is going public. Should I invest in the initial public offering (IPO)?

If you had bought Google (GOOG) at its IPO in August of 2004 at about $80 per share, you might feel pretty smart right now. As of this writing (late summer of 2017), GOOG (now known as Alphabet) is trading at around $915 per share. That's more than a 1,000 percent return over thirteen years. Unfortunately, very few companies see price gains like Google. One time, a friend talked me into investing in a start-up oil company that was only a few bucks per share shortly after its IPO. He "guaranteed" me it would shoot up to more than $20 per share in no time. I put thousands of dollars into it, cutting into my (not fully funded) emergency fund, and I still had plenty of consumer debt that needed to be paid off. I was a fan of Dave Ramsay at the time, but my eagerness to "get rich quick" rendered me a terrible follower of his advice.

Shortly after I purchased the stock, it dropped, and it just kept dropping. Eventually, the company went bankrupt, and the stock value dropped to zero. I have no one to blame but myself. I used money I couldn't afford to lose, on a stock I didn't understand, in a market I didn't understand, on an investment strategy I didn't understand, and because of the speculative type of stock it was, I was unable to cut my losses. I can't blame the "tipster" because these types of tips are given out everywhere, usually by well-meaning people who don't know what they are talking about. There is some good information on IPOs in *Investor's Business Daily* (Investors.com). This is more of an advanced strategy, and I'd recommend having a really good understanding of more basic strategies before trying this one. If you strongly believe you've found a terrific company that may be the next Microsoft, Apple, or Netflix, and you are determined to invest in it, just be sure you only use money that won't hurt you if you lose it. Kind of like the advice you might get if you were going to Las Vegas: don't bet with "scared money," or money you can't afford to lose.

> *So I'm starting to understand the value of sidestepping market downturns using trend following like you described in your pamphlet. What if I want to get out of my ETFs if they drop below the fifty-day moving average, but I'm at work or out of town?*

This is an important question I should have answered in my original letter. You can and should implement a stop-loss order, sometimes just called a stop order or stop-on-quote order. Your investment-brokerage website can show you how to place one fairly quickly and easily. It's sometimes explained under the help or how-to tab on the investment-brokerage website, or an investment advisor at the company you use can explain it in a phone call. The stop order triggers the sale when your stock or ETF hits a certain price. Let's say Spyder S&P 500 (SPY) is trading around $246 per share, and the fifty-day moving average is at about $240. You can set your stop at 240, and if SPY shoots down while you're away, it sells automatically. The moving averages change with time, and you'll need to adjust your stop every so often, depending on the strategy you use. You can also use a stop-buy order for just the opposite situation.

> *A friend of mine said it was crazy to manage my own investments and that I should use a financial advisor. Is this true?*

This could be completely true or completely untrue, depending on what kind of person you are. It can be quite a challenge to sort through different types of financial advisors and what exactly they do. Many of them are really salespeople who are trying to talk you into whatever financial products their firm is pushing to make a commission for themselves. There are also fee-based planners who are paid a flat fee or small percentage to give you unbiased advice and work in your best interest. I believe some of the reputable investment brokerages such as Schwab offer this service to a certain degree with your account. There are also independent fee-based financial planners, but many of them have a very large minimum investment requirement. It's kind of ironic that the people who could use this service the most (young people getting started) can't get access to it.

There is one name in particular (I won't mention them for fear of getting sued) that pops up if you do a Google search in many towns. I hear of many people using them, and they're a pretty common brand name. My understanding is they steer you to their own company's mutual funds and charge very high fees of up to 4 percent in addition to high yearly management fees, regardless of whether your portfolio is doing well or not. What if your portfolio is really averaging 12 percent, but after fees you're only seeing 8 percent? Remember the example of compound interest if you invested $500 a month for thirty years? If you did that with 8 percent compounded returns, you'd end up with just over $745,000. If you did that with 12 percent compounded returns, you'd end up with around $1.747 million. That's a very large difference in the quality of your retirement.

Do you think real estate investing is a good idea?

It could be a great idea or a horrible idea, depending on your situation. I would say the key to making it a good idea would be to have some patience and make sure you are plenty knowledgeable and prepared before entering this endeavor. Purchasing a rental property or a flip property can be quite a bit more challenging and expensive than it appears. I'd strongly recommend having an additional contingency fund for unexpected repairs and expenses, in addition to all estimated down payments, closing costs, repair costs, and so forth, and in addition to your personal emergency fund. I once used my personal emergency fund to buy and fix up a house that I then planned to either sell or rent, depending on buyer interest. After I got it looking really nice and ready to sell, it was badly vandalized. I had no money left to fix it again, so I was forced to sell it to another investor for a steep loss. If I had been better prepared, it wouldn't have been such a desperate situation. I've also had a couple of experiences in which I made a little money but nothing like those flip shows on TV. I think a wisely built portfolio of rental properties could potentially be a great source of passive retirement income. A couple of books I enjoyed on this topic are *Secrets of a Millionaire Real Estate Investor*, by Robert Shemin, and *The Millionaire Real Estate Investor*, by Gary Keller.

> *I was at a social gathering where someone said that investing is wrong and supports evil corporations. Is this true?*

Are there times when companies do harm to the environment? Probably so. Are there members of corporations who engage in immoral business practices? Sure. However, I'd say most companies are led by driven people who want to provide useful products and services to consumers at a profit and in the process, create jobs and opportunities. I don't feel guilty about working hard and investing, especially considering I give a portion of my income to charity, as my spiritual faith encourages. Also, the products and services I buy contribute to someone having a job. I tend to wish for the best for people. It makes me happy to see people have a clean place to live, a car or other useful transportation they enjoy, a job they like, enough money to pay the bills, enough money to enjoy some hobbies or entertainment, and a healthy retirement plan. Some people get jealous of or angry with people who achieve these things. I suppose all you can do is wish them well and keep up the good work.

> *You gave an example of a diversified portfolio using a buy-and-hold strategy and also gave an example of how someone might use trend following to get into and out of the market using the fifty-day moving average. Which of these do you use?*

I use a combination strategy of both. I diversify my portfolio somewhat similarly to the example I gave in the letter, devoting portions to ETFs representing US growth stocks, international stocks, US growth-and-income (sometimes referred to as value, dividend-payer, or blue-chip) stocks, and real estate investment trusts, and I devote an aggressive portion to leveraged ETFs. For the US growth stocks portion of my portfolio, I might use Schwab Large-Cap Growth (SCHG) or Vanguard Growth Index Fund (VUG). I also like Innovator IBD 50 (FFTY), which tracks the *Investor's Business Daily* top fifty stocks.

For international stocks, I might use Vanguard Total World (VT) and/or Schwab International Small/Mid Blend (SCHC). For the ETFs in the growth portion and the international portion of my portfolio, I follow the fifty-day moving average as I showed in the example in the letter. However, if the ETF I'm using crosses below the two-hundred-day moving average, I just stay out completely. This is especially true if the fifty-day moving average crosses below the two-hundred-day moving average. For the growth-and-income portion, I might use something like Schwab Dividend Equity (SCHD) or Oppenheimer Ultra Dividend Revenue (RDIV). For the real estate portion, I might use Vanguard REIT (VNQ) or Schwab US REIT (SCHH). The growth-and-income and REIT funds tend to move much more slowly and steadily, so for these types of funds, I like to follow the two-hundred-day moving average instead of the fifty-day moving average, getting in when the price moves above the two-hundred-day moving average and getting out when the price moves below the two-hundred-day moving average. If the two-hundred-day moving average ever appears to be moving downward, I just stay out completely until it appears to have turned upward again.

As for the aggressive portion of the portfolio, I use a combination of ProShares UltraPro QQQ (TQQQ) and/or ProShares UltraPro S&P 500 (UPRO) and/or ProShares UltraPro Dow (UDOW). These represent the NASDAQ, the S&P 500, and the Dow Jones indexes respectively, but they are triple leveraged. This means they are designed to move three times as much as the index moves. If the index goes up around 1 percent that day, then the triple-leveraged ETF would go up around 3 percent that day. They also go down three times as much so be sure to have stops in place, also make sure to dedicate only a reasonable portion of your portfolio to these leveraged ETFs, not to exceed about 20 percent. A big downturn in the market could really bite you in the butt, but if you are wise and careful, they can supercharge the gains in your portfolio quite a bit.

I also often add one more portion to my portfolio, dedicated to picking out some top growth stocks that I've identified using *Investor's Business Daily*, wishingwealthblog.com, or another cool membership website I like called ftmdaily.com ("ftm" for "follow the money"). If I had $6,000 dollars to invest, I'd put a thousand into each of a growth ETF, an international ETF, a growth-and-income ETF, a real estate investment trust ETF, and a leveraged ETF. With the growth, international, and leveraged ETFs, I'd make my buys and sell stops along the fifty-day moving average. With the growth-and-income and REIT ETFs, I'd follow the two-hundred-day moving average. I'd split the final $1,000 dollars into two $500 portions and pick out a couple of single stocks that I believe are potential winners, chosen using strategies from *IBD*, and so forth. I think my portfolio would perform just as well and be easier to manage if I didn't bother with trying to pick out winning single stocks, but I find it kind of fun. There are many times a portion or multiple portions of my portfolio get stopped out and are in cash as I wait for the proper buying opportunity to get back in. In a major market downturn, it's very likely I'd be in all cash. A prudent investor might want to divide his or her portfolio further and add a portion to represent the bond market and/or precious metals. I personally don't bother with these, but I believe I will as I get older and feel the need to be more cautious and diversified.

CHAPTER 4
CONCLUSION

When I went back and added a few more definitions and answered a few more questions, I started thinking about many more I could add. I then remembered that this short book is meant to be a fairly brief overview of the most important concepts I've learned over many years of trial and error. This booklet might be enough for you to get started implementing and managing your own portfolio of ETFs or mutual funds using a long-term buy-and-hold strategy. You might also decide to add in a bit of trend-following strategy to try to sidestep the major market downturns. You might decide you'd rather not think about these kinds of things and get an advisor to manage your investment account. Who knows? This letter might serve to tickle your investing bone and act as the tip of the iceberg on your investing education journey toward becoming a trading and investing wiz!